BINGO WITH THE INDIANS

Adam Rapp

BROADWAY PLAY PUBLISHING INC
New York
www.broadwayplaypublishing.com
info@broadwayplaypublishing.com

BINGO WITH THE INDIANS
© Copyright 2008 by Adam Rapp

Cover art by Elizabeth Kandel
1st printing: December 2008
I S B N: 978-0-88145-404-8

Book design: Marie Donovan
Word processing: Microsoft Word
Typographic controls: Ventura Publisher
Typeface: Palatino
Printed and bound in the U S A

BINGO WITH THE INDIANS was first produced
by The Flea Theater (Jim Simpson, Artistic Director;
Carol Ostrow, Producing Director) from 25 October-
22 December 2007. The cast and creative contributors
were as follows:

STASH ....Cooper Daniels
DEE ....Jessica Pohly
WILSON ....Rob Yang
STEVE .... Evan Enderle
MRS WOOD.....................Missel Leddington
GIRL/JACKSON .... Corinne Donly
NATIVE AMERICAN MAN .... Ben Horner

Director ....Adam Rapp
Assistant director ....Jessica Fisch
Stage manager ....Rachel Sterner
Set design .... John McDermott
Lighting design .... Miranda Hardy
Costume design ....Daphne Javitch
Sound design .... Brandon Wolcott
Press .... Ron Lasko/Spin Cycle
Equipment & support .... Technical Artistry

(*A cheap motel room. Two beds. Simple furnishings.*
DEE *is seated at a small table, loading a gun. She wears
Army fatigue pants and combat boots. She is thirty-ish, hard.
In front of her is a cylinder of insect repellant and a gun
cleaning kit.* STASH, *thirty-ish, nervous, overly-caffeinnated,
thin and edgy, is sitting on the toilet, wearing a black ski
mask. He wears black jeans with an enormous turquoise
belt buckle, a tight-fitting cowboy shirt, and cowboy boots.
His pinkies are painted with black nail polish.* WILSON,
*thirty-ish, younger, quietly sneaky, is lying on the bed,
reading, wearing a black wig and glasses, a mag light
flashlight on the bedside table.*)

STASH: How much time we got?

DEE: A while.

STASH: What's a while mean?

DEE: It means we may go sooner we may go later,
depends on when we get the call.

STASH: And who's calling again?

DEE: My cousin.

STASH: Your cousin.

DEE: Yeah, Phyllis.

STASH: And when is Phyllis supposed to call exactly?

DEE: She'll call when she calls, you fucking boner.

STASH: And you actually know this cousin Phyllis?

DEE: Of course I know this cousin Phyllis. We used to
go canoeing together. Brownies, shit like that.

STASH: *(Entering from bathroom, rubbing toothpaste on his gums)* I lost my cherry to a Brownie. A third-grader. I was in fifth. She was tight, man. *(Looking out the window)* Where the fuck are we, anyway?

DEE: It's called New Hampshire.

STASH: It's so dark here.

DEE: We're in the mountains, man. It gets dark.

STASH: My cellphone doesn't even work.

DEE: Thank God. You and your cellphone. All you do is check your voicemail.

STASH: I had a really good audition yesterday.

DEE: You have a really good audition every day, Stash.

STASH: I might get a call back.

DEE: For what, another spear-carrier?

STASH: No, not another spear-carrier, Dee. I'd play an astronaut. He's on stage the whole second act.

DEE: As what, a chess piece? A potted plant?

STASH: He moves, he has dialogue.

DEE: A message for you ma'am. Have a nice evening.

STASH: He speaks in verse, okay?

DEE: Verse what kind of verse.

STASH: In like iambic fucking pentameter.

DEE: For what theatre?

STASH: They're called Dogwater Productions. They're new.

DEE: Everyone's new. Everyone's new and everyone's no one. What space are they using?

WILSON: They don't have a space.

DEE: Of course they don't have a space! Nobody has a fucking space!

STASH: At the audition they said they might be doing it site specific.

DEE: Where?

STASH: In that vacant lot on Fourteenth Street. The one next to that ninety-nine cents store. There's a pate of concrete. It's a perfect playing space.

DEE: That lot with all the rubble?

STASH: They'll clear the rubble.

DEE: No, *you'll* clear the rubble, Stash. You'll be the company rubble clearer. Can't you just see it, Wilson? Stash in an astronaut suit, barking out his lines while shoveling carparts and shattered glass?

WILSON: Hah.

STASH: *(Running back into the bathroom)* Fat sloppy bitch.

DEE: Skinny hopeless larva.

STASH: Dyke.

DEE: Faggit.

STASH: Cow.

DEE: Worm.

(WILSON *fake farts like a French horn.*)

DEE: My sentiments exactly. Thank you, Wilson. What the fuck is a *pate*, anyway?

STASH: A pate's a pate. It's like a slab.

DEE: How does one perform on a slab?

STASH: *(Entering from bathroom, clutching his sides)* Think patio. Or deck. Or fucking veranda, you unimaginative pig.

DEE: I suppose there's nudity in this "patio" play, too...
Are the folks from Dogwater Productions talking
nudity?

STASH: They said there might be.

DEE: Jesus Christ. Who is this agent you're freelancing
with anyway?

WILSON: He's not an agent.

DEE: Well what the fuck is he?

STASH: He's sort of a manager. A manager slash lawyer.

WILSON: Slash landlord.

STASH: Slash landlord, so what?

DEE: Slash child molester.

STASH: He knows people.

DEE: And where did you meet him, on the subway?

WILSON: He met him online.

STASH: Gee, thanks, Wilson.

DEE: You met him in a fucking chat room?

STASH: What does it matter where I met him? He's
connected and he's helping me. He's sent me out
on like five things.

DEE: Yeah, and they all require nudity and one project
may or may not be a fucking snuff film involving
certain weird construction workers from Sarajevo.
(Throws STASH *a black turtleneck)* What's his name,
anyway?

STASH: *(Changing his shirt)* Timber.

DEE: Timber?

STASH: Yeah, Timber.

DEE: Like *Timber* Timber?

STASH: Timber like when you fucking chop down a tree timber.

DEE: Timber what?

STASH: Timber Dick.

DEE: Timber *Dick*?

STASH: Yeah, Timber Dick.

DEE: What the fuck is that?

STASH: It's his name.

DEE: He sounds like a porn star. Or a fucking warlock or something.

STASH: *(Suddenly attacked with athlete's foot itch)* He's fucking connected, okay?!!!

DEE: Connected to what, those weirdos from Sarajevo?

STASH: Well, you gotta start somewhere, you walking venereal wart.

DEE: Stash, why do you think we're here, man?

STASH: I DON'T KNOW, DEE! WHY *ARE* WE HERE?! I MEAN WE RENTED A FUCKING CAR. WE DROVE HALF THE DAY!!!

DEE: SIT DOWN! RIGHT THERE!

(STASH *sits.*)

DEE: I just happen to be the most underappreciated young director in New York and you just happen to be one of the most underappreciated writer-performers below Fourteenth Street and it's time to take matters into our own hands. Man the fucking gunboats of destiny, right Wilson?

WILSON: *(Flat)* Woo-ha.

STASH: How much do you think we'll come away with, anyway?

DEE: Well, it's five bucks for a bingo card. Phyllis
said that a lot of people buy three or four cards,
so conservatively speaking that's ten bucks a pop.
With three hundred heads it's an easy triple.

   For nine hundred bucks Van says we can rent that
theater on East Fourth Street for a week, and that
includes air conditioning and free use of the light and
sound boards. We also need to hire a publicist, rent
a proper rehearsal space, make postcards, and get you
a fucking decent haircut. But with three grand it's all
do-able, man. Plus it's really closer to four cause I have
an additional eight bills from temping and you said you
have three or four from working the shitter at Scores.

STASH: I don't have it any more.

DEE: Why not?

WILSON: He spent it.

DEE: You fucking spent it?

STASH: Yeah.

DEE: On what?

STASH: A watch.

DEE: You blew four hundred bucks on a watch?

STASH: It wasn't four hundred. It was more like
one-forty.

DEE: For a *watch*?

STASH: Yeah, for a watch.

DEE: Why?

STASH: I needed one.

DEE: For what?

STASH: For that astronaut audition.

DEE: Stash, sometimes I think your stupidity is infinite.

WILSON: *Infinite, infinite, infinite...*

STASH: In the breakdown it said the character was obsessed with an expensive timepiece. He's into relativity and time travel. I thought it would be a good idea to work with a prop.

DEE: So instead of buying one out of a gumball machine you opt for luxury.

STASH: I wanted it to be real, okay?

DEE: You're such a fucking prop whore.

STASH: Oh, tongue-fuck my ass, you skanky carnivorous whale.

WILSON: *(Pointing as* STASH's *feet)* RAT! ...RAT! ...RAT!

*(*STASH *scrambles around, terrified for his life until he realizes it's a joke.* WILSON *honks evilly.)*

STASH: *(In the corner now)* Wilson, come on man, you can't keep doing this. You know I hate rats.

DEE: *(Approaching* STASH *in the corner)* It must be a nice watch, huh, Wilson?

WILSON: Takes a licking but keeps on ticking.

STASH: It's a fucking Movado, okay?

DEE: Where is it?

STASH: What.

DEE: The watch. I'd like to see it.

STASH: I don't have it anymore.

DEE: Why not?

WILSON: He sold it.

STASH: Close your gash, Wilson.

DEE: You sold it?

STASH: Yeah, I sold it.

DEE: To who?

STASH: To this guy on the Bowery.

DEE: What guy on the Bowery?

WILSON: This like six-six West Indian dude. Ask him how much he got for it.

STASH: *(To* WILSON*)* You pathetic sack of menstrual drip.

DEE: How much did you get for it, Stash?

WILSON: He got forty bucks for it. The guy wanted to give him fifty but Gerald the Genius didn't have any change.

STASH: I hate you, Wilson. Someday I'm gonna rape you in your sleep with a screwdriver.

WILSON: You should just use your dick.

DEE: So what I'm actually hearing is that you sold the Movado for a hundred bucks less than what you bought it for.

WILSON: Those are the facts.

DEE: Brilliant.

STASH: *(Getting out of the corner)* Oh, teabag my nuts you fat cunt.

DEE: Why didn't you just return it?

WILSON: He lost the receipt.

DEE: Of course he lost the receipt. He'd lose his asshole if it wasn't screwed into the middle of his face.

(STASH whips his penis out.)

STASH: I'm gonna piss on you later, skankfest.

DEE: Oh yeah? Later when?

STASH: When you're asleep.

DEE: I'll make sure to wake up for it.

(STASH *wiggles his penis at* WILSON.)

WILSON: Is that like supposed to be your dick?

STASH: Well it's not a facsimile, my little Asian enigma. (*He stuffs his penis back in his pants.*)

DEE: So where's the forty bucks, Stash? The forty bucks you got for the Movado.

STASH: I used it already.

DEE: You *used* it?

STASH: Yeah, I used it.

DEE: You mean you *spent* it.

STASH: Spent it used it blew it, whatever.

DEE: Yeah, you blew it, all right. You blew it up your nose you cokehead.

STASH: Fuck you, Dee.

DEE: Fuck me?

STASH: Yeah, clean my gun you flabby-titted ho.

DEE: SIT DOWN AND ASSUME THE POSITION!

(STASH *sits on the other bed, clasps his hands in his lap.* DEE *approaches.*)

DEE: That was our production money, Stash.

STASH: It was *my* money. I'm the one who stands in a fucking bathroom for eight hours a clip for our quote-unquote *play.*

DEE: Did you even get a callback for that thing?

STASH: What thing?

DEE: The astronaut verse adventure.

STASH: Not yet.

DEE: Not yet means no.

STASH: Don't be so reassuring you might shrivel up and become attractive.

DEE: You gotta knock it off with this coke habit, Stash.

STASH: I'll knock your tits off is what I'll knock off you fucking worthless gorilla.

DEE: First it's poppers, then it's ex and now it's coke.

WILSON: Don't forget about the airplane glue.

STASH: It wasn't airplane glue it was Scotch Guard.

DEE: You're gonna be smoking crack by next Thursday. Just cause your mother licked your zits and strapped one on when you were in the fifth grade doesn't mean you have to turn all pathetic and skid row.

STASH: Just cause your father fished your fat-ass out of the Atlantic cause he thought you were a two-ton flounder doesn't mean you have to assume the responsibility of being the most notorious cunt alive.

DEE: Scotch Guard is so ghetto, man.

STASH: Your vagina is so ghetto, *man*.

DEE: I'm serious, Stash. When we get into rehearsals you can't be all hopped up on shit. You're too talented. It hurts me to see you like this. It hurts Wilson, too. Doesn't it hurt, Wilson?

WILSON: Yeah, I'm in pain.

STASH: Fuck you, Wilson.

WILSON: Bring it on, Tom Selleck.

(STASH *crosses to the window, pushes the drapes aside, peers out.)*

STASH: Man, it's so dark you can't even see past the parking lot. Are those supposed to be trees? Talk about fucking ominous.

DEE: They're black pine. The same trees you'll find in the Hurtgen Forest in Germany.

STASH: What the fuck is the Hurtgen Forest?

DEE: Oh, it's only perhaps the bloodiest battleground in World War II.

STASH: And who are you, fucking Colonel Blow-my-tits?

DEE: In late November and early December, the Fifth Armored was mired in the bitter and ill-considered Battle for The Hurtgen Forest. The Division was committed piecemeal and often used like blind Malaysian children to bolster infantry division units that had been decimated in earlier fighting. This combined with the dense, black-pine forest prevented the trademark coordinated attacks at which the division excelled. Instead, each gain of a few yards exacted a frightful price in dead and wounded. That month in the Hurtgen Forest was the darkest period in the division's combat history. Men were so hungry they ate their own hands. The thick black pine provided a dense and very Hitchcockian battle scene. I had to stage the fucker for my college thesis. It was the bloodiest motherfucking stage in the history of Traverse City Community College, was it not, Wilson?

WILSON: The bloodiest in history.

DEE: Forty percent of the Forty-sixth A I B were casualties in the attack on Hill Four-oh-one. You wanna talk paper-*maché*? You wanna talk hiring seven different carpenters to get the right angle for the Brandenberg-Bergstien Ridge? You wanna talk recruiting and costuming seventy-four non-drama-major freshmen? Or how about thirty gallons of stage

blood in one solitary, very historical performance?
Would you like to talk about that, Stash, cause we
could talk about that, couldn't we Wilson.

WILSON: We could definitely talk about that.

STASH: I didn't ask for a fucking blow-by-blow of
your undergraduate obsession with the war.

DEE: Black Pine, man! Those trees out there are black
pine! The same trees in the Hurtgen Forest! Don't you
think that's a little cool? New Hampshire? Germany?
Our mission? A strange, magical connection?

STASH: You're one of the weirdest dykes I know, Dee.
You should be wearing a fucking coonskin cap or some
shit. I was simply making a comment about the trees.
The same way one would make a comment about a
pond or a fucking woodchuck.

DEE: You know, Stash, if you put that kind of passion
into the investigation of *your* work you would probably
have a killer career by now. It pisses me off.

STASH: What pisses you off?

DEE: I don't have your talent. Your looks. I'm a director.

(STASH *slaps his neck.*)

STASH: Fucking mosquitoes every six seconds.

DEE: Use the Cutter.

STASH: Fuck that, man. That's like bathing in rat poison.

DEE: Wilson and I used the Cutter and we haven't been
bitten once, have we Wilson?

WILSON: Nary a bite.

STASH: Yeah, your skin probably tastes like arsenic.
And at this point I don't know which one of you I'm
fucking tonight but whoever's the lucky one is going

to take a shower first I'll tell you that right now boys and girls.

WILSON: Promises, promises.

STASH: You know what your eyes look like, Wilson? They look like two little colorless anuses. And when I get through skullfucking you they're gonna be all sad and stretched out and it's gonna feel so good.

WILSON: When you say things like that it makes me want to go hang gliding.

STASH: Oh, you two are so lame. You get me hot and then you both peter out like a couple of geriatrics. *(In the mirror)* I look like a fucking mime. Put your hands over your heads ladies and gentlemen and don't you dare move I'm about to run with an umbrella in a windstorm.

WILSON: Hey Stash.

(STASH turns to him.)

WILSON: *(Pointing at his feet)* RAT! ...RAT! ...RAT!

(Again, STASH scrambles for his life, retreats to the bathroom, slamming the door. WILSON and DEE share a smile. The bathroom door opens.)

STASH: Bro, please stop doing that.

WILSON: Okay.

(STASH comes out of the bathroom, wary of a rat.)

STASH: Let's go over the thing again, Dee.

DEE: I'm tired of going over it.

STASH: Come on, humor me. We get the call. Wilson stays here. We drive over to the place. We kill the lights a block away, put the car in neutral, roll into the parking lot.

DEE: You mean *you* kill the lights, *you* put the car in neutral, *you* roll into the parking lot. I'm not driving. I drove all fucking day.

STASH: We mask. You take your fat ass in the front door. I slip through the back window.

DEE: The window with the blue frame, not the one with the Dixie Cups.

STASH: The window with the blue frame. Old blue paint peeling like cancer, I know.

DEE: The one with the Dixie Cups is too small, you'll get stuck.

STASH: No, *you'll* get stuck, tubby. I probably won't get stuck. What's the name of this church, anyway?

DEE: Saint Rose of Lima.

STASH: It's a Catholic church?

DEE: Yep.

STASH: You were raised Catholic?

DEE: Yes I was.

STASH: I fucking hate Catholics. God's such a dick.

(*A knock at the door. Everyone freezes. DEE moves the guns to her lap. STASH opens a drawer, hides the masks. Another knock*)

DEE: Who's there?

STEVE: (*Off*) Um. It's Steve.

DEE: Steve who?

STEVE: (*Off*) I work in the office. You forgot your car keys.

(DEE *motions to* WILSON. *He rises off the bed, exits to the bathroom, re-enters sans the black wig and glasses, crosses to the entrance, opens the door.* STEVE *stands in the entrance.*

He is nineteen, tall, impressionable. He wears a white T-shirt and jeans. Timberland boots. He holds out a set of keys from a rental car. WILSON *takes the keys, tosses them to* DEE, *closes the door, crosses back to his bed, sits.)*

STEVE: Hey...I'm Steve.

STASH: Hi, Steve. I'm Brick.

STEVE: Hey, Brick.

STASH: That's Big Daddy, and the slightly asexual spammish-looking thing over there on the bed is Mulldoon.

STEVE: Hey, Big Daddy. Hey, Mulldoon.

WILSON: Hey, Steve.

STEVE: You guys are from New York, huh?

STASH: Yes we are, Steve. We're from New York and we're really weird.

STEVE: Cool.

STASH: Do you like weird?

STEVE: Sure.

STASH: Are you a weirdo?

STEVE: Um. I don't know.

STASH: Where are you from?

STEVE: Around here.

STASH: Ooooh, you're from Nowhereville. That would make you a Nowherevillian. Are there lots of nice happy houses in Nowhereville?

STEVE: I guess.

STASH: And do you live in one of these nice, happy houses?

STEVE: I live here actually. In the motel. In that blue house that's sort of attached to the office. My mom, my dad and me. Hey, are there like a lot of knife fights in New York?

DEE/WILSON: Blades on every corner, bro.

STASH: Yeah, blades.

STEVE: (To DEE) I think I know you. You used to live here. You were in class with my sister, right? You're Deanne.

DEE: My name's Big Daddy.

STEVE: No it's not. It's Deanne McCrackin. You were like this total theatre freak. You directed that really weird production of Joseph where all the brothers carried taser guns. You set it in this huge World War Two trench. You were friends with my sister Jane. You got in trouble cause Joseph got like voltage poisoning and pooped on the stage.

STASH: You had Joseph poop on the stage?

STEVE: Yeah, he pooped right in the trench while one of his brothers was being disemboweled by a German soldier. It was so cool. When you left town everyone thought you went away to prison.

DEE: Well now I'm Big Daddy and I live in New York.

STEVE: Jane got killed in a car accident.... You guys used to play Monkeys records in the basement. And once you painted my face red and told me I was your period. And my mom caught you guys taking a shower together...in Unit Four. She always thought you were really smart but my dad said you were a freak. Do you still do theatre?

DEE: Yeah, I still do theatre.

STEVE: What kind of stuff? I only ask cause I'm sort of secretly interested.

DEE: Well the three of us are actually creating a show together. That's why we're here.

STEVE: Are you going to like perform it at the community center or something?

DEE: No, we're just spending the night. We're on our way to um—

WILSON: Dartmouth.

DEE: Yeah, we're on our way to Dartmouth for this weeklong workshop.

STEVE: Cool. What's the play like about?

DEE: It's about everything you could possibly imagine. I'm the director. Brick performs in it. Mulldoon is my assistant.

WILSON: Stage Manager.

STASH: Gopher.

WILSON: UNION FUCKING STAGE MANAGER!

(Awkward pause)

STEVE: I've been writing a play.

DEE: Really.

STEVE: Yeah, really.

WILSON: What's it about?

STEVE: Um. Sea Monkeys, actually. It's called Breakfast with Sea Monkeys.

WILSON: Cool title.

STEVE: Thanks, Mulldoon. It's pretty different. Nothing really happens. It's sort of like *2001: A Space Odyssey*. Well, at least until the Sea Monkeys come. It's only a one-act but I think there's some pretty good stuff in it.

STASH: Aren't sea monkeys those little microscopic fishfood people?

STEVE: Um. Sort of.

STASH: Doesn't that present certain casting problems?

STEVE: Well, I wouldn't be able to use *actual* Sea Monkeys, Brick. The play's more about the kid who sends away for them, anyway. How he sort of disappears into their kingdom.

WILSON: Otherness.

STEVE: Yeah, it's pretty dark.

DEE: Darkness.

STEVE: Darkness is cool.

STASH: Voodoo bloodsport.

STEVE: What's that?

STASH: Nothing. How old are you Steve?

STEVE: Nineteen, why?

STASH: What does a lanky, slightly effeminate nineteen-year-old do in this town for pleasure?

STEVE: I'm not effeminate.

STASH: No you're right. What does a wildly butch nineteen year-old stud muffin do in this town for pleasure?

STEVE: Not much, really. Read. Rent movies. Get fucked up.

STASH: And how does one get fucked up in Nowhereville?

STEVE: Well, I tend to drink a lot of Robitussin but there's this guy who sells stuff at the Shell station. Evil Ed.

STASH: What kind of stuff does Evil Ed sell exactly?

STEVE: Crystal meth. Coke. Ecstasy. Pretty much everything.

STASH: Evil Ed, huh?

STEVE: Yeah, he's originally from Waco, Texas. He's short and squatty. Kind of a zitty face. He fought in the Gulf War.

STASH: Ooooh, a drug-dealing veteran. We should set him up with Big Daddy. Does your mom have anything?

STEVE: Like food?

STASH: Like drugs, sporto. Is her medicine chest full of chickenshit and fuck-all?

STEVE: Um. I don't know what that means.

STASH: Does she got any Valium? Any Nembutal? Any goodies from the pharmacy?

STEVE: Yeah, but it's not that kinda stuff.

STASH: What kind of stuff is it?

STEVE: Stuff for like depression or whatever.

(STASH *caws like a crow three times*.)

STEVE: My drama teacher lived in New York. He does this one-man show about rats. He used to perform it at Saint Mark's Church on the Bowery.

DEE: Saint Mark's Church isn't on the Bowery.

STEVE: It's not?

WILSON: It's on Second Avenue.

STEVE: Oh... Yeah, Kent's great. You guys would probably really like him.

STASH: Kent?

STEVE: My drama teacher. Well, he used to be. In high school.

STASH: Does Kent's one-man show start out 'Twas the night before murder and all down my pants not a crotch crab was stirring, nary a dance'?

STEVE: Um. No.

STASH: I DIDN'T THINK SO!

(WILSON *baas like a sheep. Awkward*)

STEVE: Yeah, a lot of people play Bingo around here, too.

STASH: You're kidding!

STEVE: No, I'm not. I'm totally not kidding, Brick. It's sort of the local pastime. Big Daddy would know about that. They Bingo over at the church three times a week.

STASH: Bingo as a verb. Wowzers.

STEVE: Sometimes like four hundred people play. They come from all over. They say it's the best game around. They're playing tonight, actually. The church is supposed to be busing in like three hundred Abenaki Indians from some Reservation.

WILSON: Double wowzers.

STEVE: Yeah, they just showed this video of the Abenaki down at the community center. Like fishing for salmon and doing rain dances and stuff. Man, Indians are totally into theatre. They like wear costumes twenty-four seven. Do you guys have any weed?

STASH: Aren't you a little young for that kind of thing?

STEVE: I get high.

STASH: Do you, Steve?

STEVE: Sure, Brick.

STASH: Are you a high-wire act?

STEVE: I'm just interested in stuff is all.

STASH: You're interested.

STEVE: Sure.

STASH: In stuff.

STEVE: Yeah.

STASH: What kind of stuff are you interested in, Stevorino?

STEVE: I don't know. What's your play called?

STASH: It's called *Scrape My Colon, colon, The Ballad of The Turd Burglar.*

STEVE: Turd Burglar?

STASH: Uh-huh.

STEVE: Like *turd* turd?

STASH: Like feces, man. Like doody. Like boo-boo surprise.

STEVE: Cool name.

STASH: Cool playwright.

STEVE: It sounds avant-garde. What's it about?

STASH: It's about a pedophile homosexual psychopath who can't stop smelling pussy.

STEVE: Pussy?

STASH: Yeah, pussy. You ever smelled pussy before?

STEVE: Sure.

STASH: It's also about prison rape and how the guy turns into this H I V hitman. Some of it is rapped.

STEVE: Like *rap* rapped?

STASH: Yeah, Mulldoon over there does a pretty mean beatbox.

STEVE: Excellent. And you're directing it Deanne— I mean Big Daddy?

DEE: I am the director, yes. And it's not purely
scatological. The rap is the play within the play.
The actual narrative is about a priest named Father
Diego Canterbury and how he keeps being visited
by Masha, Irena, and Olga from Chekhov's *Three Sisters*.
A conflation of the high-brow and the low-brow.
Because we're evolving, right Mulldoon?

WILSON: We evolve like the garden slug.

STASH: But the prison part's the good shit.

DEE/STASH/WILSON: FORTY DAYS AND FORTY
NIGHTS! CLUTCH THOSE BARS AND BARK LIKE
A DOG!

(WILSON barks twice.)

STEVE: Are you guys like rehearsing and stuff?

STASH: We took today off. They're repairing my honey
wagon over at the University.

DEE: But we're waiting for our evening rehearsal call.

WILSON: We're doing mask exercises tonight.

STEVE: Mask exercises?

WILSON: We all have many faces, Steve.

STEVE: Whoa. Can I watch?

DEE: Our rehearsals are sort of private. At this point
we're not even allowing Mulldoon in the room.
It's a very intimate and dangerous process.

STEVE: That's so cool! You're like doing theater!
Making shit happen!

STASH: Haven't you ever made shit happen, Steve?

STEVE: I was in Peter Pan once. I played John. They
put me in this harness and I got to fly. The girl playing
Wendy fell and broke her knees so they had to like
totally cancel the show... I'd like to come to New York.

WILSON: Come.

STEVE: Smoke a blunt. Ride in a taxi. Hey, Brick, do you like have a headshot?

STASH: Yeah, I got a headshot.

STEVE: Can I see it?

STASH: You wanna see my headshot?

STEVE: If it's cool.

STASH: Do you want to like fuck me or something? Cause this is getting a little weird, man.

STEVE: No, I just—

STASH: You wanna memorize my *resumé*? You interested in having me over to your little blue house for a *callback*? Put your hand in front of your face.

STEVE: Why.

STASH: Just do it! I wanna teach you something about acting!

WILSON: Don't do it.

STASH: Do it.

WILSON: It's a trick, Steve.

STASH: Do it, fuckface!

STEVE: Okay. *(He hesitates.)*

STASH: I'm not gonna hurt you, pretty.

(STEVE lifts his hand to his face. STASH pokes it into his nose and honks evilly. STEVE falls down.)

STASH: What is that, a watch?

(STASH grabs STEVE's wrist, removes a watch then puts the watch on his own wrist, turns it in the light.)

STASH: Nice, huh?

STEVE: Sure.

STASH: Are you a butt bandit, Steve?

STEVE: What?

STASH: Are you eager for my anus?

STEVE: Um. No.

WILSON: Leave him alone Brick.

STASH: Some little dodo bird is a hundred thousand in the hole, man, and I'm lookin around and I'm only seeing one dodo bird.

STEVE: What?

STASH: Do you want to see my jazzhole, little brother? Cause I'll sit right on your face you Howdy-Doody virgin faggit! I'll skullfuck you right through your eyes, man! I'll splooge in your brainpan so your nightmares are nice and warm and gooey!

(The phone rings three times. DEE answers it. STASH runs into the bathroom, drops to his knees.)

DEE: Hello? ...Hey, Phyllis... I'm good, thanks... Yeah, just for the night... Uh-huh... Uh-huh... Thanks for the call.

(DEE hangs up. STASH dry heaves twice.)

STEVE: I know Phyllis.

DEE: No you don't.

STEVE: Sure I do. She works at Sbarro's Pizza. She's your cousin, right?

DEE: My name is Big Daddy and I have no relatives. I was born under a tree in the Hurtgen Forest. A two-hundred-year-old black pine. I was raised by German timberwolves. I eat bark and the innards of small rodents. Close your eyes.

(STEVE *closes his eyes.* DEE *fixes the guns in her pants.*)

DEE: *(To* STASH*)* Ready to go, tough guy?

STASH: Yeah, I'm ready. Everything cool?

DEE: You tell me.

STASH: I'm cool.

DEE: Good. Give him his watch back.

STASH: Why.

DEE: Because I said so.

STEVE: My mom gave me that watch. It was a graduation present.

STASH: Well, that's just sweet as a fucking donut. What's it worth to you?

STEVE: I don't know. Nothing.

STASH: Whattaya know boys and girls, it's a Movado! I'll bet it's worth at least one-forty.

STEVE: Can I like open my eyes now?

DEE: Open your eyes, Steve.

(STEVE *opens his eyes.*)

DEE: Brick, give him the watch and let's go, man. We're gonna be late.

STASH: I'm not giving it back!

(DEE *crosses to* STASH *and punches him in the stomach.* STASH *doubles over, slides down the wall.* DEE *holds her hand out for the watch.* STASH *hands it to her. She hands it back to* STEVE.)

DEE: The rehearsal masks.

(STASH *rises off the floor, crosses to the drawer, removes two of the black ski masks.*)

STASH: Fucking mosquitoes.

(STASH *and* DEE *exit.* WILSON *remains in the bed.*
STEVE *stands awkwardly.*)

WILSON: You okay?

STEVE: Yeah, I'm cool.

WILSON: Don't mind him.

STEVE: He's pretty uptight, huh?

WILSON: Big bark. Very little bite.

(*Awkward pause*)

STEVE: Well, I should probably get going. I gotta
go vacuum unit four.

WILSON: Stay.

STEVE: Really?

WILSON: Yeah. I could use the company.

STEVE: Okay. (*He pulls out a chair, sits, then stands,
then sits.*) So you're a stage manager?

WILSON: I am.

STEVE: Is that like fun?

WILSON: It is fun. But I do other things, too.

STEVE: Like what?

WILSON: I write.

STEVE: Like plays?

WILSON: Uh-huh.

STEVE: What kinda stuff?

WILSON: You're curious aren't you?

STEVE: I guess.

WILSON: Not much to do around here, huh?

STEVE: Not really. I was supposed to go to college this year but my mom's been sort of freaking out since my sister died.

WILSON: Do you like her?

STEVE: Who, my sister?

WILSON: Your mom.

STEVE: Yeah, she's cool. She's just a little fucked up is all. She keeps packing my lunch like I'm still in the fourth grade. If I leave the motel she starts totally losing her shit.

WILSON: Does she know about your interest in theater?

STEVE: Not really.

WILSON: And your dad?

STEVE: He's the sheriff.

WILSON: I assume he's not a big theater freak.

STEVE: He used to go to my sister's shows. But he's mostly into *jai alai* and Bingo. He's probably over at the church right now.

WILSON: Really.

STEVE: Yeah, it's his night off. He's way into the community. He sort of likes everyone to feel safe.

WILSON: Is his name like Buzz or something?

STEVE: It's Brad actually.

WILSON: Brad the Dad.

STEVE: He gives me the creeps to tell you the truth. He's always preaching about saying No to drugs and all of that right wing Christian bullshit. He wants me to be a Navy Seal.

WILSON: Dad knows best.

STEVE: So is your real name Mulldoon, or is that like a stage name?

WILSON: My real name's Wilson.

STEVE: Like the cigarette.

WILSON: You like cigarettes?

STEVE: I like pot mostly. You don't have any do you?

WILSON: I do, actually. Wanna smoke some?

STEVE: Totally.

(WILSON removes a one-hitter from his pocket, loads it, passes it to STEVE, hands him a lighter. STEVE takes a hit, passes it back.)

STEVE: Cool one-hitter.

(WILSON takes a hit, exhales.)

WILSON: Another?

STEVE: Sure.

(STEVE takes another hit, hands it back to WILSON. STEVE is standing now.)

WILSON: *(Offering the chair)* Man your canoe, Davey Crockett.

(They giggle and STEVE sits.)

STEVE: So what's your play about?

WILSON: It's actually about two guys who meet in a cheap motel.

STEVE: Really?

WILSON: Yeah, really. I wrote a scene earlier today. Do you want to read it with me?

STEVE: Like *read it* read it?

WILSON: Sure.

STEVE: Yeah, I'll read it with you.

WILSON: Cool.

(WILSON *produces a script, hands it to* STEVE.)

STEVE: Don't you need a script, too?

WILSON: I'm pretty sure I got it memorized. I'll call for line if I need to.

STEVE: ...This is kick-ass pot.

WILSON: I'm glad you like it.

STEVE: It's so heady.

(STEVE *laughs.* WILSON *laughs too.*)

STEVE: So, who do you like want me to read?

WILSON: I'll read Slash, you read Wilton.

STEVE: *I'm* Wilton?

WILSON: Yeah, you read Wilton.

STEVE: You sure you don't want to read Wilton? I mean cause of how his name is so close to yours or whatever?

WILSON: I'm sure. I'll be Slash. That makes sense, right? ...Before we start I'd like to do an exercise. Would you be into that?

STEVE: Like a vocal warm-up? I know about vocal warm-ups cause my sister used to do them. Red leather yellow leather and all that.

WILSON: Well, this exercise is more like a communication thing. So we can get energetically connected. It's called Smile Unsmile. The way it works is I say, "Smile". I sort of command it. And then you hold the smile until I say, "Unsmile".Then you stop smiling. Pretty easy, huh?

(STEVE *laughs.* WILSON *laughs. They are stoned and
laugh for a bit. Just as their laughter dies,* WILSON *says,*
"Raspberries!" and they laugh more.)

WILSON: So you go first.

STEVE: I *smile* first?

WILSON: Yeah, you smile first. Ready? Take a deep
breath, then we'll start.

(STEVE *takes a deep breath.)*

WILSON: *Smiiiiiiiiiiiiiiile.*

(STEVE *smiles woodenly, holds it with a great effort.)*

WILSON: *Unsmiiiiiiiiiiiile.*

(STEVE *exhales, relieved.)*

WILSON: That was great.

STEVE: That was so weird, man. You commanded me
to smile and I like totally did it.

WILSON: Funny how that works, huh?

STEVE: I so love theatre games.

WILSON: Excellent. Now it's my turn. Whenever you're
ready. Just give me the command.

STEVE: Okay... *Smiiiiiiiiiiiiiiile.*

(WILSON *smiles, holds it.)*

STEVE: *Unsmiiiiiiiiiiiile.*

(WILSON *exhales, releases his smile.)*

STEVE: Wow! Did I do it right?

WILSON: It was perfect.

STEVE: You were so like committed.

WILSON: Thanks. Ready to act?

STEVE: Totally. Any advice?

WILSON: Just keep it simple. Connect the thoughts and say the words.

STEVE: Connect the thoughts and say the words. Right on. So I'm Wilton.

WILSON: And I'm Slash.

STEVE: Slash and Wilton. Such cool names! We're like these total characters! Theater's such a fucking trip, man!

WILSON: Well, you have the first line, so whenever you're ready.

(STEVE *clears his throat, starts acting from the script.*)

STEVE: So in the lounge you said you thought I was black?

WILSON: I never said that.

STEVE: Sure you did. When I was at the jukebox. I was looking at the C D cover for the Alan Parsons Project and you said you thought I was black.

WILSON: I said you have a nice back.

STEVE: You did?

WILSON: Yeah, bro. So can I see that turquoise belt buckle you were bragging about?

STEVE: *(Breaking from the script)* Should I like *do* this? Cause I have a belt in the other room. It's not turquoise or anything but I could like totally go and get it.

WILSON: That's not necessary. You can mime it if you want.

STEVE: Right on.

WILSON: So I'll take it from a few lines back. Ready?

STEVE: Yeah, I'm ready.

WILSON: Keep it simple.

STEVE: Keep it simple, keep it simple.

WILSON: *(Back to the play)* I said you have a nice back.

STEVE: You did?

WILSON: Yeah, bro. So can I see that turquoise belt buckle you were bragging about?

STEVE: There'll be a prince to pay.

WILSON: *(Breaking)* Price.

STEVE: What?

WILSON: There'll be a price to pay. You said prince.

STEVE: Sorry.

WILSON: Take it back again. And relax.

STEVE: Relax, relax.

WILSON: Take your shoes off. Find your feet. Connect the thoughts.

STEVE: Find my feet. Connect the thoughts. Cool, cool.

WILSON: Ready.

STEVE: Yeah, I'm ready.

WILSON: *And!*

(STEVE jumps. WILSON laughs. Their laughter gets huge again. Just as their laughter dies, STEVE says, "Raspberries!" but to no avail. Awkward.)

WILSON: I said you have a nice back.

STEVE: *(Back to the script)* You did?

WILSON: Yeah, bro. So can I see that turquoise belt buckle you were bragging about?

STEVE: There'll be a price to pay.

WILSON: Oh yeah, what kind of price?

STEVE: One that I'm not sure you can handle. Are you a big spender?

WILSON: I've been known to carry around a fair amount of cash on my person. I'll give you twenty bucks to see your belt buckle.

STEVE: That can be arranged.

WILSON: And another hundred to see your ass.

STEVE: *(Breaking)* Wait a minute. Is this like gay?

WILSON: I don't know yet. What do you think?

STEVE: I can't really tell.

WILSON: Keep going.

STEVE: Well, it says he takes his pants down.

WILSON: So?

STEVE: Should I like take my pants down?

WILSON: If you want to. I personally like it when actors go to the mountain.

(STEVE hesitates.)

WILSON: What's wrong?

STEVE: I don't know.

WILSON: You're uncomfortable.

STEVE: A little.

WILSON: You have a girlfriend.

STEVE: Well, sort of. We're kind of like, seeing other people.

WILSON: What's her name?

STEVE: Angie.

WILSON: Nice name.

STEVE: Thanks. I mean. Well, Angie would say thanks.

WILSON: She's pretty, huh?

STEVE: Yeah she's pretty. She's got these eyes. They like do stuff to you. And she that kind of red hair—

WILSON: That kind of red hair you can see a mile away.

STEVE: Yes! Exactly! I wrote a song about that exact phenomenon, man! How did you know that?

WILSON: You broke up with her or she broke up with you?

STEVE: She broke up with me, I guess. Sort of.

WILSON: What happened?

STEVE: Well, it's a little embarrassing.

WILSON: Believe me, Steve, I've been there.

STEVE: Okay, dude, I'm gonna tell you but you gotta promise not to fuck with me. Cause I'm like totally stoned right now and I might freak out and get paranoid.

WILSON: I promise I won't fuck with you, Steve.

STEVE: She wants to experiment with chicks.

WILSON: That's it?

STEVE: Yeah. Pretty weird, right?

WILSON: Not really. Every girl goes through that phase.

STEVE: They do?

WILSON: Yeah, man. They watch a few pornos, smell their own cunts on their fingers and jump on the other side of the fence for five minutes. Once they've blown a few bull-dykes they usually come back.

STEVE: Really?

WILSON: Nine times out of ten. We're mammals, Steve.

STEVE: Right on. So you think Angie'll come back?

WILSON: Absolutely.

STEVE: She says she's moving to New York.

WILSON: Oh yeah, when's she leaving?

STEVE: Next week. I'm gonna follow her. I already packed a duffel bag.

WILSON: Where is she tonight?

STEVE: She's at the bingo game, actually, which sort of freaks me out a little.

WILSON: Why does that freak you out?

STEVE: Well cause a lot of the local dykes hang there.

WILSON: Then she'll probably be back sooner than you think. Let's continue the scene, shall we?

STEVE: Oh yeah. Sure.

WILSON: And keep your hair out of your face.... Here.

(WILSON *produces a bobby pin.* STEVE *pins his bangs.*)

WILSON: In the theatre it's really important to see the actor's face.

STEVE: Right on.

WILSON: You have a nice face.

STEVE: Thanks.

WILSON: ...The scene.

STEVE: *(Back to the script)* So in the lounge you said you thought I was black?

WILSON: I never said that.

STEVE: Sure you did. When I was at the jukebox. I was looking at the C D cover for the Alan Parsons Project and you said you thought I was black.

WILSON: I said you have a nice back.

STEVE: You did?

WILSON: Yeah, bro. So can I see that turquoise belt buckle you were bragging about?

STEVE: There'll be a price to pay.

WILSON: Oh yeah, what kind of price?

STEVE: One that I'm not sure you can handle. Are you a big spender?

WILSON: I've been known to carry around a fair amount of cash on my person. I'll give you twenty bucks to see your belt buckle.

STEVE: That can be arranged.

WILSON: And another hundred to see your ass.

(STEVE *turns away, awkwardly lowers his jeans and underwear.*)

WILSON: Nice butt.

STEVE: What?

WILSON: Nice butt, it's in the script.

STEVE: Oh, right on.

WILSON: And you say...

STEVE: Um *(Back to the script)* Thanks. I get paid a king's ransom for this butt.

WILSON: Can I touch it?

STEVE: Huh?

WILSON: Can I touch it?

STEVE: Is that in the script, too?

WILSON: Not yet but it might be. Can I touch it? I'd like to.

STEVE: I know karate, dude.

WILSON: I love karate.

STEVE: I'm a brown belt.

WILSON: You gonna use it on me? ...Let me touch your butt, Steve.

STEVE: Wilton.

WILSON: Let me touch your butt, Wilton. Come on, man. Angie won't mind. She'd probably like it. *You'll* like it.

STEVE: I will?

WILSON: Sure. I won't tell anyone. Don't you trust me?

STEVE: I trust you... Slash.

WILSON: Well back up, then.

(STEVE *backs up toward* WILSON, *finding each step.* WILSON *begins fondling him.)*

WILSON: How's that? You like that?

STEVE: Yeah.

WILSON: You sure?

STEVE: Uh-huh.

WILSON: We can stop the scene if you want to. Should I stop the scene?

STEVE: Um, no.

WILSON: You ever do anything like this before, Steve?

STEVE: No.

WILSON: I'll bet Angie would love it, wouldn't she?

STEVE: Maybe.

WILSON: What about your dad? What would your dad think if he saw us?

STEVE: Um, he'd be like pissed.

WILSON: Would he shoot us?

STEVE: Probably.

WILSON: And what about your mom?

STEVE: She'd freak out.

WILSON: Would she shoot us?

STEVE: She'd probably start crying.

WILSON: Well, that's cause she loves you so much. Does mommy love you, Steve?

STEVE: Yeah.

WILSON: Are you a bad boy?

STEVE: *(Dropping the script)* Um, sometimes.

WILSON: What happens to bad boys in Nowhereville? Do they get spanked?

STEVE: Maybe.

WILSON: Do you think I should spank you?

STEVE: I don't know.

(WILSON *spanks* STEVE.)

WILSON: Are you gonna be a good boy?

STEVE: I'll be good.

(WILSON *spanks him again.*)

WILSON: If you're a good boy I'll grant you a wish.

STEVE: You will?

WILSON: Yes I will. Cause I'm like a genie. You get one wish.

(WILSON *spanks* STEVE.)

WILSON: What's it gonna be, Steve?

STEVE: What, my wish?

WILSON: Yeah, your wish.

STEVE: Um. Take me to New York with you.

WILSON: Would you like that?

STEVE: Yes.

WILSON: Would that make you the happiest boy in the world?

STEVE: Yes.

WILSON: Say it.

STEVE: It would make me the happiest boy in the world.

WILSON: Louder.

STEVE: It would make me the happiest boy in the world!

WILSON: Again.

STEVE: It would make me the happiest boy in the world! *(He starts to cry.)*

WILSON: Pull your pants up, bad boy

(STEVE pulls his pants up, turns and faces WILSON.)

WILSON: Smile!

(STEVE smiles.)

WILSON: Unsmile!

(STEVE swallows his smile.)

WILSON: Again. Smile!

(STEVE smiles.)

WILSON: Unsmile!

(STEVE swallows his smile.)

WILSON: I'll take you to New York.

STEVE: You will?

WILSON: Yes, Steve, I will. But only if you're good.

STEVE: Good at what?

(WILSON *approaches him and they kiss against the bureau. It gets sort of intense. After a moment,* WILSON *flips* STEVE *onto his stomach.* STEVE *is facing the bureau now,* WILSON*starts to take his pants off.*)

STEVE: Can we do this in the bathroom? ...Please?

WILSON: Okay.

(*They go into the bathroom, leaving the door ajar. A moment later* STEVE *cries out. Pleasure. Pain. Confusion. Strange, animal desperation. The bathroom door is slammed shut. Erotic descent. Brief flight. Annihilation.* STEVE *emerges from the bathroom, pulling his pants and underwear up.* WILSON *follows.*)

WILSON: You okay?

STEVE: Uh-huh.

WILSON: Don't you want to finish this?

STEVE: Sure.

WILSON: Well come here then.

(STEVE *crosses to* WILSON *and* WILSON *gently takes* STEVE'*s clothes off, then his own. He pushes* STEVE *to the floor near the foot of the bed. They continue fucking. After four of five thrusts the front door opens.* MRS WOOD, STEVE'*s mother, materializes at the door. She wears a robe and slippers. Her hair is tousled. She is mid-forties, disoriented, depressed.*)

MRS WOOD: Steven?

(STEVE *quickly scrambles into his jeans and T-shirt, briefly sitting on the bed.* WILSON *gets into the bed naked.*)

MRS WOOD: Steven, is that you?

STEVE: (*Getting into the T-shirt*) Mom, what are you doing?

MRS WOOD: What's going on in here?

STEVE: Nothing.

MRS WOOD: It's after nine pm, Steven.

STEVE: So?

MRS WOOD: So it's getting late.

STEVE: Nine's not late, Mom.

MRS WOOD: Who is that?

STEVE: Just a friend.

MRS WOOD: What kind of friend?

STEVE: The kind of friend who you like meet.

WILSON: *(Waving)* Hidy.

MRS WOOD: I don't think I know this friend. Where'd you meet him?

STEVE: I just met him. It's cool, okay?

MRS WOOD: Okay.

(WILSON slaps his neck.)

STEVE: Mom, close the door, you're letting all the mosquitoes in.

(MRS WOOD closes the door, stays facing the door.)

MRS WOOD: Do I smell marijuana in here?

STEVE: No.

MRS WOOD: Steven, honey, if you're smoking marijuana again I'll be very disappointed. And so will your father.

STEVE: I'm not smoking marijuana, Mom, I swear. That was Unit Seven.

MRS WOOD: Are you sure?

STEVE: Yes!

MRS WOOD: That nice couple from Boston?

STEVE: Total stoners, Mom. They were playing this game called "Smile Unsmile."

WILSON: Big time stoner game.

STEVE: I already knocked on their door and warned em.

MRS WOOD: It's awfully late to be having friends visiting.

STEVE: What, I can't have friends now?

MRS WOOD: Of course you can have friends, honey.

STEVE: Just fucking chill. Jesus.

MRS WOOD: You know I hate it when you use than language, Stevie. It breaks my heart.

STEVE: Go to bed.

MRS WOOD: Maybe I don't want to go to bed. Maybe I need your help with something.

STEVE: What.

MRS WOOD: Well, the candy machine is jammed and there have been several complaints.

STEVE: There have not.

MRS WOOD: There most certainly have been. This nice young man from unit seven left a note.

STEVE: So open it up and fix it. You have a key. You know how to do it.

MRS WOOD: I'd like you to do it.

STEVE: Later, okay?

MRS WOOD: You never know who's going to want a snack in the middle of the night.

STEVE: Mom, nobody's gonna want a snack in the middle of the night. Get with the times, yo.

MRS WOOD: I'm with the times.

STEVE: Yeah, right.

(MRS WOOD *starts to cry.*)

STEVE: Mom, don't fucking cry!

MRS WOOD: *(Crying)* I'm not.

STEVE: Yes you are, man. You're totally blubbering.

MRS WOOD: *(Crying)* Well, what in the world is going on in here?

STEVE: Nothing, okay?

MRS WOOD: *(Crying)* Stevie, if your father was here I'm sure he'd find it awfully peculiar.

STEVE: So don't tell him... We're just hanging out. Stop crying.

MRS WOOD: What's his name, anyway?

STEVE: Why?!

MRS WOOD: Because it isn't polite to not introduce people to your mother.

STEVE: It's Mulldoon, okay?

MRS WOOD: Okay.

STEVE: Mulldoon, as you've prolly figured out by now, this is my moms.

MRS WOOD: And what's my name?

STEVE: Um. Donna Wood.

(Barechested, WILSON *gets out of bed revealing a bloodstain where* STEVE *had briefly sat. Keeping a blanket wrapped around his waist,* WILSON *approaches* MRS WOOD, *extends his hand.*)

WILSON: Pleased to meet you, Donna.

MRS WOOD: Nice to meet you, too, Mulldoon...
What is that in your hair, Steven?

STEVE: *(Removing the bobby pin)* Nothing. It's nothing.

(WILSON sits on other bed.)

MRS WOOD: And what are you boys doing in here
exactly?

WILSON: We're working on stuff.

STEVE: Yeah, we're like totally working on stuff.

MRS WOOD: What kind of stuff?

WILSON: Just stuff.

STEVE: Yeah, just *stuff*, okay?! And we're not boys!

MRS WOOD: Okay. There's no reason to get hostile
with me, Steven.

STEVE: Well, can't I work on *stuff*?!

MRS WOOD: Of course, honey.

STEVE: Is *stuff* suddenly like illegal or something?

WILSON: We're actually making theater, Donna.

MRS WOOD: You are?

WILSON: Thespian storytelling at its most cutting edge.

STEVE: It's so cutting edge it's practically illegal.

WILSON: There's not even a proper word for it.

STEVE: It's like *diamond-edged*, Mom. That's about as
close as you can get to naming it.

WILSON: It's an elusive and powerful drama, Donna.
Red leather, yellow leather and suchlike. Your son is
quite talented.

MRS WOOD: Oh. Well, I know Steven has expressed
some interest in acting, but I had no idea he was
exploring it in any way.... Oh my god.

STEVE: What now?

MRS WOOD: The sheet.

STEVE: What sheet?

MRS WOOD: The flat sheet on that bed. The one next to Milton. There's blood on it.

STEVE: Dude, you are so tripping. And it's *Mulldoon.*

MRS WOOD: THERE IS BLOOD ALL OVER THAT SHEET, STEVEN!

WILSON: There's no reason to be alarmed, Donna. It's stage blood.

MRS WOOD: It is?

WILSON: Red food coloring and Karo corn syrup. Looks just like the real thing.

STEVE: Mulldoon is a professional stage manager, Mom.

WILSON: *(Proffering the sheet)* Wanna taste it? I can do brains and feces, too.

MRS WOOD: Oh dear. No, thank you.

WILSON: Donna, I know it looks like something strange is happening in here, but I can assure you that there is nothing to worry about. This is all part of the magic of the theatre. Art imitates life and vice versa. Your fears and concerns are completely valid. What we do as theater artists is strive for authenticity, thereby blurring the line between illusion and reality. It's through this investigation that we arrive at catharsis and when that happens all of us, both the performers and the members of the audience—the entire theatrical community— are transformed, are imbued with empathy and ultimately come to a fuller understanding of what it means to be human.

MRS WOOD: Well, I've never really thought about it like that.

WILSON: Would you like to join us? We could always use another company member.

MRS WOOD: Oh dear, no thank you, Mulldoon. It sounds really interesting but I'm afraid I have terrible stage fright. If you'll excuse me for a moment, I'm afraid I need to use the bathroom.

(MRS WOOD *exits to the bathroom.* WILSON *covers the bloodstain, quickly gets dressed. As* STEVE *hands him his shirt:)*

WILSON: You're amazing.

(The front door opens and DEE *enters with a* GIRL. *She is nineteen, pretty. She has dyed black boyish hair and a nose ring. She wears long jeans shorts, a white tank top and a black three-quarter boots.* DEE *is not wearing her mask. She is holding an enormous butterball turkey and an answering machine still in the box.* DEE *closes the door.)*

STEVE: Angie?

GIRL: Excuse me?

STEVE: Angie, it's me—Steve.

GIRL: I'm not Angie.

STEVE: *(A joke)* Oh. You're not?

GIRL: Who the fuck is Angie?

DEE: Wilson, Steve, this is Jackson.

(DEE *throws turkey to* WILSON.*)*

GIRL: What's up?

STEVE: That's not Jackson. Her name is Angie Fripple.

DEE: She looks like a Jackson to me. We met at the Bingo game. At the lesbian table, right Jackson?

GIRL: At the hardcore table, actually.

DEE: She has a great ass and she's hardcore.

STEVE: Since when are you hardcore?

WILSON: The room is aswim with queers.

STEVE: I'm not queer.

WILSON: Ha.

GIRL: I am. I'm fucking queer as a red-nosed reindeer.

DEE: You and Steve here should get to know each other.

GIRL: I don't want to know him.

STEVE: Angie, what the fuck?

GIRL: JACKSON!

STEVE: *(To* WILSON *and* DEE*)* She's totally tripping.

DEE: She seems pretty fucking lucid to me.

STEVE: *(To* GIRL*)* Dude, what did you do to your hair? She used to have long red hair. It was the kind of red hair—

WILSON: That you could see a mile away. You wrote a song about it.

STEVE: That's not her hair!

DEE: Looks like her hair to me.

STEVE: When did you get the nose ring?

DEE: She has a pierced clit, too, right, Jackson?

GIRL: Sterling silver stud. I did my nipples, too.

STEVE: You did?

WILSON: She's hardcore.

DEE: I'd say.

GIRL: I'm doing my tongue next week.

STEVE: This is a joke, right?

GIRL: You're a fucking joke. All breeders eat red meat and die of dick cancer.

WILSON: Palpable uncertainty regarding the breeder factor.

STEVE: She's into fucking Shanaya Twain and the Dixie Chicks! We ate cheese dogs at Dave's American Red Hots just three days ago! She has a poster of Brad Pitt above her bed! We have turquoise peace rings that we bought in Montreal last summer! *(He brandishes his ringed finger.)* We got Expos hats, too! Look at her finger!

GIRL: I've never seen this person before in my life.

STEVE: She's totally lying. We dated for like four years. This is all an act. *(To the* GIRL*)* Don't you know who that is? That's Deanne McCrackin. She's from here. She was my sister's...friend.

GIRL: Her name is Big Daddy and she's from New York City.

(The GIRL *kisses* DEE. *Its' a real kiss.* MRS WOOD *enters from the bathroom, now wearing* WILSON*'s wig from the top of the play.*

MRS WOOD: Angie Fripple, what on earth did you do to your hair?

STEVE: Meet my moms, everyone.

MRS WOOD: You had such beautiful long red hair, Angie.

GIRL: That's not my name.

WILSON: Her name is Jackson.

MRS WOOD: And what did you do to your poor nose? Is that a shark's tooth?

STEVE: Mom!

MRS WOOD: What, Steven?

STEVE: Can't you see that you're in the way here, man? You like totally ambushed this oasis of artistic discovery.

WILSON: We're living as our characters and writing about it as we go, Donna.

STEVE: He's Slash and I'm Wilton. And that's Big Daddy and Jackson.

MRS WOOD: I thought you said his name was Mulldoon.

STEVE: It is Mulldoon. But his character name is Slash.

MRS WOOD: Oh.

STEVE: Get with the program, bro.

(WILSON *holds up the answering machine.*)

WILSON: We even have props.

STEVE: Yeah, we totally have props.

WILSON: And a working script.

STEVE: That script totally works, Mom.

WILSON: *(Pulling out the gun from under the pillow.)* Fake Colt Forty-five revolver. Top of the line stage weapon. Wanna touch it?

MRS WOOD: Oh dear. No, thank you.

(WILSON *slides the gun back under the pillow.*)

MRS WOOD: Deanne McCrackin, is that you?

DEE: Hello, Mrs. Wood.

MRS WOOD: Oh my god. I didn't know you were back in town. I saw your dad the other day at church. He didn't mention you were coming home.

DEE: I'm just passing through. I'm working on an important project that requires lots of field research.

MRS WOOD: But I'm sure he would love to see you. You know he had to have part of his leg removed. He's had just the hardest time. His diabetes got pretty unmanageable the past year or so. It's so sad. You know how he loved to fish and bowl. You should drop in and see him... What kind of a project are you working on?

WILSON: Motel theatre project.

STEVE: She's the director.

DEE: Artistic Director, actually.

MRS WOOD: Well, that sounds official.

DEE: Yeah, Me and the members of my company have been traveling around to different motels in the rural northeast. We're developing a theatre piece based on our experience. It's being funded by the New York Foundation for the Arts.

WILSON: NY-FA to the rescue.

MRS WOOD: Well, that all sounds very interesting.

STEVE: It's sorta like top secret, Mom.

WILSON: Very hush hush.

STEVE: So you can't tell anyone. Especially Dad.

MRS WOOD: Oh, I won't breathe a word... And how do you fit into this, Angie?

GIRL: Jackson.

MRS WOOD: I mean Jackson.

DEE: She's our newly hired intern.

GIRL: I'm moving to New York City. I'm leaving tonight.

MRS WOOD: Angie, does your father know about this?

GIRL: My name is Jackson and I no longer have a father.

STEVE: She's in character, Mom.

MRS WOOD: ...Deanne—

STEVE: Big Daddy!

MRS WOOD: Big Daddy, did you know that Jane died last year?

DEE: I know. I was sorry to hear that, Mrs Wood.

MRS WOOD: Right out there on I-Ninety-three. Head on collision. She was on her way to New York.

STEVE: Jesus...

MRS WOOD: Sometimes I still think I can hear her cleaning the units. But then I'll open the door and nobody's there. *(To* DEE*)* I know how you two were, well *close*. *(To* WILSON*)* Jane and Deanne were, well close.

STEVE: Mom, go back to bed. I'll be home in a little while.

MRS WOOD: She met a man here at the motel. His name was Jack Curry and he was from New York City. He worked in the Chrysler Building. An insurance salesman. He drove a big blue car. I'll never forget watching it pulling out of the lot. How the gravel sounded...
    I begged her to stay, but she wouldn't listen. She really admired you, Deanne. She was always sad that you never came home.

DEE: Well, it would have been nice to see her again, Mrs. Wood.

MRS WOOD: I'm glad to hear that you're still involved with the theatre. You were always so creative.

DEE: I've been busy developing my company in New York.

WILSON: There's a good chance that Steve here is going to be a part of it.

MRS WOOD: Oh, well that's exciting. I hope it's
something he can do from here.

DEE: We're actually about to begin a very important
rehearsal, Mrs. Wood.

STEVE: It's been this total like balls-out collaboration,
Mom. It's about these two dudes who meet in the bar
of a cheap motel.

DEE: Your son has been a big help.

WILSON: Indeed he has.

STEVE: Thanks, guys. It's been such an honor.

MRS WOOD: It's a funny thing, the theatre. The
audience. The lights. When someone starts crying
on stage is it real? Sometimes you just don't know.
    Once I saw a man die on stage. His character had
cancer. You could see the makeup and the fake bald
cap and everything. But after the curtain fell I got
the feeling that I was never going to see him again.
It was Dick Boudreaux from the pie shop. I even
stopped ordering pies for Thanksgiving because
I was afraid I would go to the shop to pick it up and
he wouldn't be there.
    And I don't think I've ever been in a place that can get
so dark. When the lights go out it's the strangest feeling.
Sometimes you can't even see your own hand in front
of your face. Sometimes it can be so real... (*She has faded
off somehow, holding her hand in front of her face.*)

(STASH *enters, cocaine encrusting the rim of his nostrils and
mustache. He starts to perform his solo piece,* Scrape my
Colon, colon, The Ballad of the Turd Burglar. *He is
incredibly animated, sharp, at times physically explosive.
Some or all of the piece might be rapped.*)

STASH: Twas the night before murder
and all down my pants

not a crotch crab was stirring,
nary a dance.

Not the B-boys from B-ville
or the pimps from Pampoon,
not the crackheads from Cracktown
or the Mons from Monsoon.

I got in my Caddy
and headed downtown.
I was lookin for turds,
on a bend from some brown.

It's the Burglar! The Burglar!
the Burglar! they screamed.
It's the Burglar from Turd Town
and he's hungry for cream.

Plug up your bungholes
and chainlink your slacks
His turd bucket's empty!
He's coming, think fast!

The playground was hot, man,
the tin slide was gleaming.
Fresh-diapered children
were pooping and screaming.

What toddlers! What babies!
What tikes full of dook!
I held high my bucket.
Such babes, what a fluke!

The sun was a sausage.
The sky was all gravy.
Laxative birds!
My knees were all wavy!

A two-year-old redhead
was playing with sand.
Her diapers were droopy
with booboo—how grand.

Come hither young Judy.
Your mommy's no lookie.
I'll burgle your turds
and give you a cookie.

Salerno or Tollhouse
or Keebler, feel free.
Fudge stripes and wafers
and powdered pralines!

Her hand was so small;
her fingers just dainty
Don't fear my sweet Judy
Just lend me your panties

The raging brown joy
of poop pedophilia.
Carnivorous hunger!
Such sweet sensamilia!

So I gave her a cookie
and she slid them right off.
A diaper so soiled,
perhaps one was enough.

But just as her turds
were burgled just right,
a cop grabbed my bucket
and ruined the night!

Oh, Officer Friendly!
Oh, Good Sergeant Billy!
I'm harmless, I *love* kids!
Don't be so silly!

But he took me straight in
and locked me up tight.
He smashed my poor bucket!
The world wasn't right!

It was lockdown at Downtown.
I was lowdown and dirty.

But I couldn't be crushed!
I was just too damn flirty!

There were white men and black men
and boys with big muscles.
But their turds wouldn't budge
without a good hustle—

(STASH *strips down to his underwear, exits briefly to the
bathroom, returns with a toy horse on a stick. It is also
obvious now that he is clutching a large baggie of cocaine.
He tosses the horse to* WILSON, *starts to hustle, faster and
faster, the cocaine flying everywhere. An orgy of cocaine.
He then suddenly collapses, convulses, passes out, the bag
of cocaine on his chest.*)

MRS WOOD: Are we still doing theatre, or is this real?

WILSON: The question of the night.

MRS WOOD: Does he need to go to the hospital?

WILSON: He's in a deep state of creative hypnosis.

MRS WOOD: Well, he certainly is concentrating.

WILSON: He should be coming out of it in a few
minutes, right Big Daddy?

DEE: Two minutes tops.

STEVE: He's an actor.

WILSON: Thus the need for auto-hypnosis and other
forms of psychically charged mind conditioning.
At the end of tonight's rehearsal process there's a
good chance that all of us will be down on the floor
in that same state.

MRS WOOD: Is that an illegal substance.

STEVE: Is what an illegal substance?

MRS WOOD: The plastic bag with white powder that's
sitting on his chest.

WILSON: It's vitamin B and flour.

MRS WOOD: It is?

WILSON: It's actually good for you. Clears up the sinuses. Care for a toot?

MRS WOOD: No, thank you. I think I've seen enough. I'd better go home.

STEVE: Thank you!

MRS WOOD: I just pray that I can get to sleep tonight.

STEVE: You'll be fine. Just don't cry anymore.

(MRS WOOD *crosses to exit, stops in front of* WILSON, *removes her wig, hands it to him, he hands her the toy horse on the stick.)*

MRS WOOD: Steven, don't forget you have to get up tomorrow. That new bed for unit three is being delivered by the Kunkle brothers.

STEVE: I know.

MRS WOOD: And the plumber will be dropping by an invoice for the work he did in the laundry room. We'll need you to sign off on it because I have to go into town for my appointment. *(To the* GIRL*)* It was nice to run into you again, Angie.

GIRL: Jackson.

MRS WOOD: I mean Jackson. I've missed seeing you around the motel. And Deanne, I'll be sure to give your regards to your father. He'll be happy to know that you were in town.

DEE: Thanks, Mrs Wood.

MRS WOOD: Steven, if you see your father—

STEVE: Mom, please...

MRS WOOD: Goodbye everyone.

(MRS WOOD *exits. The sound of a car passing in the distance*)

STEVE: Sorry about that. She's a little fucked up since Jane... Well, you heard what happened... *(Looking around)*But that was so great, right? ...All that stuff about hypnosis and the creative process... And the whole thing about the vitamin B and flour! That totally rocked, Wilson. I mean Mulldoon. I mean... And Red leather yellow leather and all that! We were like totally collaborating, right Angie?! I mean Jackson.

(The GIRL removes a cigarette, lights it, starts smoking.)

STEVE: When did you start smoking, anyway? You used to hate it when I smoked.

WILSON: *(To DEE)* So what happened at Bingo?

DEE: What happened was I come busting through the basement doors at St. Rose of Lima's as planned and I hear O-forty-seven, O-forty-seven, O-forty-seven, I'm fully masked, packing fire, and I'm sweatin like a Christmas pig.

I got my eye on the cashbox. Little plywood, slatted thing thick with twenties and tens. I'm about to start barking out orders when this malarial-looking, turtlenecked motherfucker springs to his feet and yells—

GIRL: Bingo.

DEE: Guess who it is?

WILSON: Tom Selleck I mean Yani I mean Stash.

DEE: Stash the motherfucking Gash. He's jumping up and down so hard I think his eyes are gonna pop out. He's got like four Bingo cards in front of him, and he's surrounded by Indians.

GIRL: It was Abenaki Indian Night.

DEE: Oh, was it ever.

GIRL: They bused them in from some reservation.

WILSON: So Stash wins.

DEE: He wins? Ha! The worm scores three grand and a Panasonic Platinum portable stereo!

GIRL: It was the bonus game. They always offer Panasonic merchandise at the bonus game. Mister Webster from the Best Buy in Montpellier is a bigtime player.

DEE: You shoulda seen it, Wilson. I couldn't even stage a freakier scene. Three hundred fucking Abenaki's, man.

GIRL: They're really into denim.

DEE: And Nike cross-trainers.

GIRL: And Allen Iverson.

DEE: I win a butterball turkey and an answering machine and Stash makes off with the goddamn crown jewels.

WILSON: So where's the money?

DEE: Well, apparently, Stash paid a little visit to Evil Ed at the Shell Station and scored a shitload of fucking coke!

GIRL: He spent our fucking play money.

WILSON: What should we do?

DEE: I say this calls for a company fight call.

WILSON: You think?

DEE: I totally think. The motherfucker gets what he deserves. Call it, Wilson.

WILSON: My pleasure. (*He produces a stopwatch.*)

WILSON: COMPANY FIGHT CALL! COMPANY FIGHT CALL—THIRTY SECONDS!

DEE: Thank you, thirty seconds.

GIRL: Thank you, thirty seconds.

WILSON: *(Lacing up his combat boots)* I can't believe this. We come all this way. How many hours did we drive?

DEE: Half the day.

WILSON: Half the fucking day. *(Checking his stopwatch)* COMPANY FIGHT CALL. COMPANY FIGHT CALL—TWENTY SECONDS!

DEE: Thank you, twenty seconds.

GIRL: Thank you, twenty seconds.

DEE: *(Lacing up her combat boots)* And we pull the motherfucker off *legally! Legal money*, Wilson! It's too bad, isn't it? Just when it all seemed like things were finally coming together.

WILSON: *(Checking his stopwatch)* COMPANY FIGHT CALL! COMPANY FIGHT CALL —TEN SECONDS!

DEE: Thank you, ten seconds.

GIRL: Thank you, ten seconds.

STEVE: *(To GIRL)* What happens in ten seconds?

DEE: All that talent. Those looks. I only wish I was so lucky.

(WILSON quickly moves to STASH.)

WILSON: *(Reading stopwatch)* COMPANY FIGHT CALL! COMPANY FIGHT CALL! T-minus five, four, three, two, one.

(WILSON kicks STASH violently in the ribs several times. STASH comes to. On all fours, he starts to crawl away. DEE comes up behind him, grabs the back of his head, rears back and slams his head into the floor. Pleading for his life, he tries to escape to the bathroom, but before he can get the door closed, DEE stops it with her foot.)

DEE: *MAG LIGHT!*

(WILSON *retrieves the flashlight and they both enter the bathroom, the door slamming behind them. We hear the sounds of them beating* STASH *with the flashlight. It is savage. They re-enter,* WILSON *holding the flashlight. He offers it to the room and the* GIRL *takes it, enters the bathroom, picks up from where they left off. Again, this is brutal. She returns, holding the flashlight, staring at* STEVE.)

DEE: Fight call's a full-company activity, Steve. There are no exceptions.

STEVE: Did you just really hit him, Angie?

GIRL: Jackson!

STEVE: I mean Jackson. Were those hits real?

DEE: You in or not, Steevorino?

STEVE: I'm in.

DEE: Then you better show us what you're made of. Jackson here obviously doesn't mind getting her hands dirty.

GIRL: I'd like to get them filthy, actually.

DEE: It looks like we found ourselves a new company member, Wilson. In fact, I say we bypass the internship and make her an artistic associate.

WILSON: Welcome to the Big Apple, Jackson.

GIRL: I love apples. The bigger the better.

DEE: She can crash on the Equity futon.

STEVE: I can crash on the Equity futon, too.

DEE: I don't think so, Steve.

STEVE: Why not?

DEE: Because in order for little boys from the provinces to become certified company members they have to go beyond the call of duty. At this point you're not even looking at an internship, bro.

STEVE: I'm not a little boy.

WILSON: Then get to work...Wilton.

STEVE: Okay... Slash.

DEE: I might advise putting your boots on.

(STEVE *steps into his Timberland Boots. While lacing them, the* GIRL *says "Tick-tock, tick-tock, tick-tock..."* STASH *emerges from the bathroom, crawling on all fours, his face soaked in blood, barely conscious, muttering, "I'm sorry, I'm sorry, I'm sorry," under his breath. He reaches up toward* WILSON, *then collapses. The* GIRL *offers the flashlight to* STEVE. *He takes it, stands over* STASH, *looks at* WILSON, *then* DEE, *then the* GIRL. *Nobody flinches. He drops to his knees with the flashlight. Just as he is about to rear back, a* NATIVE AMERICAN MAN *enters through the front door. He holds a water drum and small mallet. He is dressed in denim and wears tennis shoes.)*

(*He sings and chants and performs a spiritual dance around* STASH's *body. As he passes each member in the room, they are filled with a kind of terrible wonder.)*

(*When the* NATIVE AMERICAN MAN *finishes his dance he exits, leaving the door open. His song and tom-tom can be heard fading in the distance over the following:)*

(STASH *wakes, slowly stands. He is in a strange delirium. He looks around the room, confused. After a moment:)*

STASH: Oh, listen to the music! They're going away. One of them has already gone away for good, we're alone, and now we have to start our lives all over again...we have to go on living...

   Someday everyone will know what this was all about, all this suffering, it won't be a mystery anymore, but until then we have to go on living...and working, just

keep on working. I'll go away tomorrow, by myself.
I'll teach school, and devote my whole life to people
who need it...who may need it. It's autumn, winter will
come, the snow will fall, and I will go on working and
working.

The music sounds so happy, so positive, it makes you
want to live. Oh dear God. The day will come when
we'll go away forever too, people will forget all about
us, they'll forget what we looked like and what our
voices sounded like and how many of us there were,
but our suffering will turn to joy for the people who
live after us, their lives will be happy and peaceful,
and they'll remember us kindly and bless us. My dears,
my dear sisters, life isn't over yet. We'll go on living.
The music sounds so happy, so joyful, it almost seems
as if a minute more, and we'd know why we live,
why we suffer. If only we knew. If only we knew!

Tara-ra-boom-der-ay, it's gonna rain today. What
difference does it make? What difference does it make?

If only we knew! If only we knew!

(STASH *kisses* DEE, STEVE, GIRL *and*WILSON *good-bye.
He then removes his clothes, slowly exits following the fading
song of the* NATIVE AMERICAN MAN. *He leaves the door
open.*)

(WILSON *crosses to the door.*)

WILSON: He's following the Indian.

DEE: Where are they going?

WILSON: Into the woods. He's following him into the
woods.

(*The sound of the distant drum fading.* WILSON *closes the
door, turns back.*)

DEE: Wilson, how's that play of yours coming along?

WILSON: Excellent, actually.

DEE: Getting the kinks out of that second act?

WILSON: I did some really good work on it just tonight, right Steve?

STEVE: Sure.

WILSON: And I think I have a pretty good bead on the ending.

DEE: Good. We'll start rehearsals next week. Let's load up and get the fuck outta here. Jackson, get the turkey and the answering machine. Wilson, make sure we're not leaving anything behind.

(DEE *throws the* GIRL *the car keys. She pockets them and collects the turkey, the answering machine, exits.*)

STEVE: What about me?

DEE: What *about* you, tiger?

STEVE: You should give me something to do.

DEE: I think we got everything covered... I'm sure there are a million things you could be doing right now that don't involve this, Steve.

STEVE: Like what?

DEE: Like anything you could possibly imagine.

(*The* GIRL *re-enters, collects* STASH's *strewn clothes, his boots, his socks and underwear, exits.*)

STEVE: I'll do anything. Please.

WILSON: Looks like we got everything.

DEE: What about the shitter, you check the shitter?

STEVE: I can check the shitter.

(DEE *and* WILSON *share a look.*)

STEVE: Let me check the shitter. I totally know how to do that.

DEE: AS YOU WERE!

STEVE: Can I check the shitter, Wilson?

WILSON: I don't think you're qualified, Steve.

STEVE: But I'm totally qualified. I like work here.

WILSON: I don't think so.

STEVE: Why not?

WILSON: Because I'm a union fucking stage manager and I say there's an egregious lack of certain qualifications. You couldn't even execute the company fight call.

STEVE: Please...

DEE: Check the shitter, Wilson.

(WILSON *exits into the bathroom, re-enters.)*

WILSON: Bathroom's all clear.

DEE: Alright, let's get the fuck outta here.

STEVE: I'll totally do the company fight call! I'll do it, Wilson, look! *(He starts to kick the wall. He kicks it nine or thirteen times. It gets a little intense. A tense pause)* Wilson, why are you doing this?

WILSON: Doing what?

STEVE: You said I could come with.

WILSON: Did I say that?

STEVE: Dude, you granted me a wish. You said you'd take me to New York. I'll go get my stuff, it'll just take a minute.

WILSON: We don't have a minute, Steve.

STEVE: Then I *won't* get my stuff. I'll just like freeball it for a few days.

WILSON: I don't think so.

STEVE: But you promised.

WILSON: I said if you were good.

STEVE: But I *was* good. I was totally amazing. You said so yourself.

WILSON: I was acting. That's what we *do* in the theater.

(The GIRL *re-enters.)*

GIRL: Anything else?

DEE: We're all set.

*(*STEVE *takes a step towards* WILSON, *his hand outstretched.* WILSON *spits in* STEVE's *face.)*

DEE: Stevie, do yourself a favor and go fix the candy machine.

*(*STEVE *takes another step toward* WILSON. WILSON *pushes him to the floor, holds him there with the gun. The* GIRL *leaves with* DEE.)*

*(*STEVE *makes another move toward* WILSON *and* WILSON *mimes shooting* STEVE, *commanding, "BANG! BANG!"* STEVE *flies over the bed, disappears, comes up a moment later, his hand outstretched in front of him, as if to protect himself.* WILSON *mimes shooting him twice more, commanding "BANG! BANG!" again.* STEVE *crashes into the corner, slides down the wall, again comes up, stunned, lurching toward* WILSON. WILSON *then fires the gun and two live shots ring out. They are blanks, but the shots drive* STEVE *backwards into the bathroom. He disappears behind the door.* WILSON *turns and exits.)*

(The sound of car doors opening and closing.)

(The sound of a car starting.)

(The sound of a car pulling away over gravel.)

*(*STEVE *crosses to the window, peers out. Headlights pan across the window, briefly filling the room with light.* STEVE

moves away from the window, takes in the room, all that has happened, turns to the audience.)

STEVE: Smile! ...Unsmile! *(A beat)* Smile! ...Unsmile!

(His legs give out and he sits on the bed. He starts to weep as lights fade to black.)

END OF PLAY

www.ingramcontent.com/pod-product-compliance
Lightning Source LLC
Chambersburg PA
CBHW052219090426
42741CB00010B/2596